COUNTRY

Formal Name: Kingdom of Thailand (Ratcha Anachak Thai). ราชอาณาจักรไทย

Short Form: Thailand (Prathet Thai—ประเทศไทย—Land of the Free, or, less formally, Muang Thai—เมืองไทย—also meaning Land of the Free; officially known from 1855 to 1939 and from 1946 to 1949 as Siam—Prathet Sayam, ประเทศสยาม, a historical name referring to people in the Chao Phraya Valley—the name used by Europeans since 1592).

Term for Citizen(s): Thai (singular and plural). พลเมือง

Capital: Bangkok (in Thai, Krung Thep, กรุงเทพ—City of Angels).

Major Cities: The largest metropolitan area is the capital, Bangkok, with an estimated 9.6 million inhabitants in 2002. According to the 2000 Thai census, 6.3 million people were living in the metropolitan area (combining Bangkok and Thon Buri). Other major cities, based on 2000 census data, include Samut Prakan (378,000), Nanthaburi (291,000), Udon Thani (220,000), and Nakhon Ratchasima (204,000). Fifteen other cities had populations of more than 100,000 in 2000.

Independence: The traditional founding date is 1238. Unlike other nations in Southeast Asia, Thailand was never colonized.

National Public Holidays: New Year's Day (January 1), Makha Bucha Day (Buddhist All Saints Day, movable date in late January to early March), Chakri Day (celebration of the current dynasty, April 6), Songkran Day (New Year's according to Thai lunar calendar, movable date in April), National Labor Day (May 1), Coronation Day (May 5), Visakha Bucha Day (Triple Anniversary Day—commemorates the birth, death, and enlightenment of Buddha, movable date in May), Asanha Bucha Day (Buddhist Monkhood Day, movable date in July), Khao Phansa (beginning of Buddhist Lent, movable date in July), Queen's Birthday (August 12), Chulalongkorn Day (birthday of King Rama V, October 23), King's Birthday—Thailand's National Day (December 5), Constitution Day (December 10), and New Year's Eve (December 31). The Thai calendar has been adapted to the Western calendar of days, weeks, and months. Years are numbered according to the Buddhist era, which commenced 543 years before the Christian era. Therefore, 2005 is the year 2548 in the Buddhist era.

Flag: Five horizontal bands of red (on top), white, blue (double width), white, and red. The red stripes represent unity of the nation, the white strips represent purity of religion, and the blue stripe in the center represents the king.

Click to Enlarge Image

HISTORICAL BACKGROUND

Prehistory: The earliest known inhabitation of present-day Thailand dates to the Paleolithic period, about 20,000 years ago. Archaeology has revealed evidence in the Khorat Plateau in the northeast of prehistoric inhabitants who may have forged bronze implements as early as 3000 B.C. and cultivated rice during the fourth millennium B.C.

Early History: In the ninth century B.C., Mon and Khmer people established kingdoms that included large areas of what is now Thailand. Much of what these people absorbed from contacts with South Asian peoples—religious, social, political, and cultural ideas and institutions—later influenced the development of Thailand's culture and national identity. In the second century B.C., the Hindu-led state of Funan in present-day Cambodia and central Thailand had close commercial contact with India and was a base for Hindu merchant-missionaries. In the southern Isthmus of Kra, Malay city-states controlled routes used by traders and travelers journeying between India and Indochina (present-day Cambodia, Laos, and Vietnam).

Nanchao Period (650–1250): Located on the southwestern border of China's Tang empire (A.D. 618–907), Nanchao served as a buffer for and later rival to China. The Tai, a people who originally lived in Nanchao, migrated into mainland Southeast Asia over a period of many centuries during the first millennium A.D.

Sukhothai Period (1238–1438): In 1238 a Tai chieftain, Sri Intraditya, declared his independence from Khmer overlords and established a kingdom at Sukhothai in the Chao Phraya Valley in central Thailand. The people of the central plain took the name *Thai*, which means "free," to distinguish themselves from other Tai people still under foreign rule. The Kingdom of Sukhothai conquered the Isthmus of Kra in the thirteenth century and financed itself with war booty and tribute from vassal states in Burma, Laos, and the Malay Peninsula. During the reign of Ramkhamhaeng (Rama the Great, r. 1279–98), Sukhothai established diplomatic relations with the Yuan Dynasty (1279–1368) in China and acknowledged China's emperor as its nominal overlord. After Ramkhamhaeng's death, the vassal states gradually broke away; a politically weakened Sukhothai was forced to submit in 1378 to the rising new Thai Kingdom of Ayutthaya and was completely absorbed by 1438.

During and following the Sukhothai period, the Thai-speaking Kingdom of Lan Na flourished in the north near the border with Burma. With its capital at Chiang Mai, the name also sometimes given to this kingdom, Lan Na emerged as an independent city-state in 1296. Later, from the sixteenth to eighteenth centuries, Lan Na came under the control of Burma.

Ayutthaya Period (1350–1767): The city-state of Ayutthaya was founded in 1350 and established its capital in 1351 on the Chao Phraya River in central Thailand, calling it Ayutthaya, after Ayodhaya, the Indian city of the hero Rama in the Hindu epic *Ramayana*. In 1360 Ramathibodi (r. 1351–69) declared Theravada Buddhism as the official religion and compiled a legal code based on Hindu legal texts and Thai custom that remained in effect until the late nineteenth century.

Ayutthaya became the region's most powerful kingdom, eventually capturing Angkor and forcing the Khmer to submit to Thai suzerainty. Rather than a unified kingdom, Ayutthaya was a patchwork of self-governing principalities and tributary provinces ruled by members of the royal family who owed allegiance to the king. The king, however, was an absolute monarch who took on god-like aspects. This belief in a divine kingship continued until the eighteenth century. The kingdom became increasingly sophisticated as new social, political, and economic developments took place.

In 1511 Ayutthaya received its first diplomatic mission from the Portuguese, who earlier that year had conquered the state of Malacca to the south. Ayutthaya concluded trade treaties with Portugal in 1516 and with the Netherlands in 1592 and established commercial ties with Japan and England in the seventeenth century. Thai diplomatic missions also went to Paris and The Hague. When the Dutch used force to extract extraterritorial rights and freer trade access in 1664, Ayutthaya turned to France for assistance in building fortifications. In addition to construction engineers, French missionaries and the first printing press soon arrived. Fear of the threat of foreign religion to Buddhism and the arrival of English warships provoked anti-European reactions in the late seventeenth century and ushered in a 150-year period of conscious isolation from contacts with the West.

After a bloody dynastic struggle in the 1690s, Ayutthaya entered what some historians have called its golden age—a relatively peaceful period in the second quarter of the eighteenth century when art, literature, and learning flourished. The rising power of Burma led to a Burmese invasion of Ayutthaya and the destruction of its capital and culture in 1767. Only a Chinese attack on Burma kept the chaotic Thai polity from Burmese subjugation.

Thon Buri Period (1767–82): The Thai made a quick recovery under the leadership of a half-Chinese military commander, Phraya Taksin. Taksin had escaped from the besieged Ayutthaya and organized resistance to the Burmese invaders, eventually driving them out. Taksin declared himself king and established a new capital at Thon Buri, a fortress town across the river from modern Bangkok. By 1774 Taksin had annexed Lan Na and reunited Ayutthaya in 1776. He was deposed and executed in 1782, however, by his ministers, who invoked interests of the state over Taksin's claim to divinity.

Early Chakri Period (1782–1868): Another general, Chakri, assumed the throne and took the name Yot Fa (Rama I, r. 1782–1809). Yot Fa established the ruling house that continues to the present. The court moved across the river to the village of Bangkok, the kingdom's economy revived, and what remained of the artistic heritage of Ayutthaya was restored. The Kingdom of Bangkok consolidated claims to territory in Cambodia and the Malayan state of Kedah while Britain annexed territory in an area that had been contested by the Thai and the Burmese for centuries. Subsequent treaties—in 1826 with Britain and in 1833 with the United States—granted foreign trade concessions in Bangkok. The kingdom's expansion was halted in all directions by 1851.

The reign of King Mongkut (Rama IV, r. 1851–68) marked a new opening to the Western nations. To avoid the humiliations suffered by China and Burma in their wars with Britain and the resulting unequal treaties, Bangkok negotiated and signed treaties with Britain, the United

States, France, and other European countries between 1855 and 1870. As a result, commerce with the West increased and, in turn, revolutionized the Thai economy and connected it to the world monetary system. Foreign demands for extraterritoriality convinced Mongkut that legal and administrative reforms were needed if Siam (as the Thai kingdom was officially known from 1855 to 1939 and from 1946 to 1949; prior to then, the Thai traditionally named their country after the capital city) were to be treated as an equal by the Western powers. Monkut's death in 1868 postponed further reforms, however.

Reign of Chulalongkorn, Reforms, and War (1868–1932): Real reform occurred during the reign of Chulalongkorn (Rama V, r. 1868–1910). After his formal enthronement in 1873, he announced reforms of the judiciary, state finance, and the political structure. An antireform revolt was suppressed in 1874, after which Chulalongkorn embarked on less radical approaches. In time, he ordered the gradual elimination of slavery and corvée labor. He introduced currency-based taxes and a conscription-based regular army. In 1893 a centralized state administration replaced the semifeudal provincial administration. The regime established European-style schools for children of the royal family and sent government officials, promising civil servants, and military officers to Europe for further education. The first railroad line was opened between Bangkok and Ayutthaya in 1897 and extended farther north in 1901 and 1909. To the south, rail connections were made in 1903, linking with British rail lines in Malaya.

During this time, British and French colonial advances in Southeast Asia posed serious threats to Siam's independence and forced Siam to relinquish its claims in Cambodia, Laos, and the northern Malay states. Although much diminished in territory by the 1910s, Siam preserved its independence, and the kingdom served as a buffer state between the British and French colonies. During this time, anti-Chinese sentiments came to the fore. About 10 percent of the population was Chinese, and ethnic Chinese largely controlled many government positions, the rice trade, and other enterprises, much to the resentment of the native Thai.

Siam joined the Allies in declaring war against Germany during World War I (1914–18) and sent a small expeditionary force to the European western front. These actions won Siam favorable amendments to its treaties with France and Britain at the end of the war. Siam also gained, as spoils of war, impounded German ships for use in its merchant marine. Siam took part in the Versailles peace conference in 1919 and was a founding member of the League of Nations.

The Emergence of Constitutional Rule (1932–41): A bloodless coup d'état in 1932, engineered by a group of Western-oriented and nationalist-minded government officials and army officers, ended the absolute monarchy and ushered in a constitutional regime. The first parliamentary elections were held in November 1933, confirming Minister of Finance Pridi Phanomyong's popularity, but Luang Plack Phibunsongkhram (Phibun) used his considerable power as minister of defense to assert the superior efficiency of the military administration over the civilian bureaucracy. In 1938 Phibun succeeded as prime minister, with Pridi continuing with the finance portfolio. The Phibun administration promoted nationalism and in 1939 officially changed the nation's name from Siam to Muang Thai (Land of the Free), or Thailand. Foreign-owned businesses (mostly Chinese-owned) were heavily taxed, and state subsidies were offered to Thai-owned enterprises. The people were encouraged to emulate European-style fashions. Betel chewing was prohibited, and opium addicts were prosecuted. Irridentist claims for lost

4

territories in Cambodia and Laos were revived amidst new anti-French sentiment. Phibun cultivated closer relations with Japan as a model for modernization and a challenge to European power.

Thailand During World War II (1941–44): After World War II broke out in Europe (1939–45), Japan used its influence with the Vichy regime in France to obtain territorial concessions for Thailand in Laos and Cambodia. The war for Thailand began in earnest on December 8, 1941, when Thai and Japanese troops clashed on the Isthmus of Kra. Bangkok acceded to Japan's demands that its troops be permitted to cross the isthmus to invade Burma and Malaya. In January 1942, Phibun signed a mutual defense pact with Japan and declared war against Britain and the United States. Seni Pramoj, the anti-Japanese Thai ambassador to Washington, refused his government's orders to deliver the declaration of war, and the United States refrained from declaring war on Thailand. Seni organized a Free Thai movement, and, with U.S. government support, Thai personnel were trained for anti-Japanese underground activities. In Thailand, Pridi ran a clandestine movement that, by the end of the war, with Allied aid had armed more than 50,000 Thai to resist the Japanese. During the early war years, Phibun was rewarded for his cooperation with Tokyo with the return of further territory that had once been under Thai control. Japan stationed some 150,000 troops in Thailand and built the infamous "death railway" across the River Kwai and through Thailand using Allied prisoners of war. The Allies bombed Bangkok during the war, and public opinion and the civilian political leaders forced Phibun out of office in June 1944.

Civilian Government (1945–47): Shortly after the war, Seni Pramoj briefly served as prime minister. In May 1946, a new constitution was promulgated. It called for a bicameral legislature with a popularly elected lower house and an upper house elected by the lower house. The name Siam was officially restored. The 1946 elections set the stage for Pridi's accession to the prime minstership. However, two weeks after the election Pridi was accused of being implicated in the untimely death of King Ananda Mahidol (Rama VIII, r. 1935–46), and he resigned and left the country. The new king, Bhumibol Adulyadej (Rama IX, r. 1946–), who was born in Cambridge, Massachusetts, in 1927, had spent the war in Switzerland and returned there after a brief first visit to Thailand in 1945. He did not return to Bangkok to take up his kingly duties until 1951, following a government-engineered coup.

Return to Military Rule (1947–73): The civilian government's failure eventually led to the restoration of the Phibun military faction. Phibun had been arrested in 1945 as a war criminal but was released soon afterward. A coup in November 1947 ousted the civilian leaders, and Phibun took over as prime minister in April 1948. During his second government (1948–57), Phibun restored the use of the name Thailand, reintroduced legislation to make Thai social behavior conform to Western standards, improved secondary education, and increased military appropriations. Phibun's traditional anticommunist position led to Thailand's continued recognition of Taiwan, and he supported the French in their actions against communist insurgents in Indochina. Thailand also provided ground, naval, and air units to the United Nations (UN) forces fighting during the Korean War (1950–53; Thai forces continued to serve in South Korea until 1972). Phibun brought Thailand into the new Southeast Asia Treaty Organization (SEATO) in 1954. In 1955 SEATO's headquarters was established in Bangkok, and Thailand offered the United States the use of Thai military bases. In an attempt to generate

5

popular support for himself, Phibun articulated a policy of democracy, but he was deposed in a bloodless coup in September 1957.

Military-controlled government continued between 1957 and 1967. There was talk under Prime Minister Sarit Thanarat of a "restoration" of the king, and a strong popular affection for the monarchy arose. The regime emphasized the kingdom's Buddhist heritage in an effort to gain support from monks for government programs. Anticommunism continued to influence Thailand's foreign affairs, and in 1961 Thailand, the Philippines, and newly independent Malaya (since 1963, Malaysia) formed the Association of Southeast Asia (ASA). In 1967 Thailand became a founding member of the Association of Southeast Asian Nations (ASEAN), a broader regional cooperative organization that replaced the ASA. At the same time, Prime Minister Thanom Kittikachorn decided to shorten the timetable for the country's transition from the military-dominated leadership structure to a popularly elected government.

In June 1968, a new constitution was proclaimed, but martial law, which had been imposed in 1958, remained in effect. Party politics resumed in 1968, and Thanom's United Thai People's Party carried the February 1969 National Assembly elections. The new government, however, had to respond to numerous issues: a Muslim insurgency in southern Thailand, communist guerrillas operating in jungle areas north of the Thai-Malaysian border, the successes of communist forces in Vietnam and Laos, and other regional unrest and protests against the government. In November 1971, Thanom carried out a coup against his own government, thereby ending the three-year experiment in parliamentary democracy. The constitution was suspended, political parties were banned, and the military took full charge in suppressing opposition.

Transition to Democratic Rule (1973–76): The stern moves by the Thanom regime led to popular dissatisfaction among university students and organized labor, accompanied by growing anti-U.S. sentiments. Some feared Thanom would even overthrow the monarchy and establish a republic. In a demonstration on October 13, 1973, some 250,000 people pressed their grievances against the government. The following day, troops fired on the demonstrators, killing 75 of them. King Bhumibol took a rare direct role, forcing the cabinet's resignation; Thanom and his close colleagues were allowed to leave the country secretly. Thammasak University president Sanya Dharmasakti was appointed interim prime minister, and it was he who fully credited the student movement with bringing down the military dictatorship. A new constitution went into effect in October 1974, providing for a popularly elected House of Representatives. The elections were inconclusive, and conservative Seni Pramoj eventually formed a government that lasted less than a month. His brother, Kukrit Pramoj, then put together a more acceptable centrist coalition that lasted until January 1976. Seni returned as prime minister but only until October 1976, when violent student demonstrations were suppressed by security forces, and Seni was ousted. A military junta took control of the government, declared martial law, annulled the constitution, banned political parties, and strictly censored the media.

Military Rule and Limited Parliamentary Government (1976–92): The new government, led by Prime Minister Thanin Kraivichien, a strident anticommunist, was more repressive in many ways than the earlier military regimes. Strict censorship continued, and the regime tightly controlled labor unions and purged suspected communists from the civil service and educational institutions. As a result, many students joined the communist insurgency. Thanin was replaced in 1977 by General Kriangsak Chomanand. He promulgated a new constitution in December 1978 with a popularly elected House of Representatives and an appointed Senate, but the military controlled cabinet and Senate appointments. Economic instability, however, brought down the Kriangsak government in March 1980. The new prime minster, who was the commander in chief of the army and minister of defense, General Prem Tinsulanonda, came to power by consensus among key politicians. He gave civilians a greater role in government by appointing civilians to his cabinet. A coup attempt in 1981 weakened Prem's government, and there was continual dissension among the civilian members of the government. Despite student and farmer demonstrations, Prem was reappointed as prime minister in April 1983. He survived a coup attempt in September 1985 and elections in July 1986. Prem was succeeded as prime minister following elections in July 1988 by General Chatichai Choonhavan, the leader of a multiparty coalition. The following years saw a series of military-led governments, efforts to reform, coups, new elections, and coalition party politics. Reforms were introduced in the business sector, the government allowed increased foreign investment, and relations with Cambodia, Laos, and Vietnam improved. Charges of corruption and abuse of power abounded, however, and Chatichai was removed from power in a bloodless coup in February 1991.

Multiparty Democracy (1992–2006): In March 1992, with a new constitution in force and new elections held, General Suchinda Kraprayoon, one of the February 1991 coup leaders, became prime minister and leader of a five-party coalition. When those parties withdrew their support, Suchinda resigned in May 1992, and Anand Panyarachun, a civilian who had served as acting prime minister between March 1991 and March 1992, was named prime minister. Anand embarked on new reform measures, but he was replaced after the September 1992 elections by Democratic Party (Phak Prachatipat) leader Chuan Leekpai, the head of a four-party coalition. Chuan's government pushed through constitutional amendments that provided for more wide-ranging democratic practices, enlarged the House of Representatives, reduced the size of the appointed Senate, lowered the voting age from 20 to 18 years of age, guaranteed equality for women, and established an administrative court. In January 1985, the Thai Nation Party (Phak Chat Thai) won the largest number of House seats, and its leader, Banharn Silapa-Archa, headed the new coalition government. In March 1996, Banharn appointed the members of the new Senate; unlike earlier Senates, most members were civilians instead of military officers. The failure of his coalition, however, led to new elections and a new six-party coalition government in November 1996 led by General Chavalit Yongchaiyudh, head of the Phak Khwam Wang Mai (New Aspiration Party).

Chavalit made key economic portfolio appointments to his cabinet, but he failed to implement the austere fiscal policies needed to revive a weak economy. In mid-1997 a major financial crisis ensued, the baht—Thailand's currency—was devalued, the Central Bank governor resigned, and widespread protests took place. The government announced austerity measures, and the International Monetary Fund (IMF) intervened, but the economy continued to deteriorate. Despite a new constitution promulgated in October 1997, confidence in Chavalit continued to slide, and elections in November returned Chuan Leekpai to the prime ministership as head of a seven-party coalition. This transfer of power without military intervention, from one elected leader to another, represented a major breakthrough in the development of democratic processes in Thailand. The baht continued to devalue, however, and social unrest recurred. By the summer of 1998, the economy had become more stable, although investigations into banking practices continued to uncover mismanagement and irregularities. With assistance from the IMF, Thailand gradually regained macroeconomic stability.

The first-ever elections to the Senate were held in 2000, and, in January 2001 one party—the Phak Thai Rak Thai (Thai Loves Thai Party)—won an absolute majority in the House of Representatives. Because of widespread allegations of illegal election practices, new polling took place in February in some constituencies. The Thai Rak Thai, having merged with another party since the January election, still won the absolute majority of seats, but a coalition government—with the New Aspiration Party and Chat Thai—was established. Police Lieutenant Colonel Thaksin Chinnawat became prime minister. The Thai Rak Thai was further strengthened in 2002 when it absorbed many members of the New Aspiration Party.

Thaksin set out to stabilize several problematic areas. One was to launch a major antidrug campaign. Some 2,275 people were killed in a three-month period ending in April 2003, and the government claimed to have eradicated 90 percent of Thailand's drug problem. In October 2004, the government launched a second antidrug campaign. Another problem confronting the kingdom was terrorist violence, primarily in the south. In 2002 several police officers were killed, bombs were detonated when the minister of interior toured the violence-prone area, and five schools suffered damage from arsonists. The Thai military attributed these actions to a group thought to be an al Qaeda affiliate and arrested suspected members of Jemaah Islamiah (Community of Islam) in June 2003. They confessed to plotting attacks on embassies in Bangkok and tourist sites. Further arsons and bombings occurred, and attacks on police and army bases in 2004 heightened the terrorist threat. In 2004 alone, more than 500 people died as a result of insurgent and terrorist violence in the south. This loss of life was exacerbated when a massive tsunami hit the Andaman coast on December 26, 2004, killing more than 5,300 Thai and foreigners and leaving another 2,900 reported missing.

In February 2005, the Thai Rak Thai won a 75 percent majority in the House of Representatives elections, and, for the first time, a single-party government was formed. The following year, however, there were mass protests calling for Thaksin's resignation over corruption issues. He called for early parliamentary elections in April 2006 that were boycotted by the major opposition parties and declared unconstitutional in May. Amidst growing protests, Thaksin continued as prime minister until September 19, 2006, when military forces staged a successful coup and set up a military-controlled regime.

GEOGRAPHY

Location: Thailand is located in the center of peninsular Southeast Asia. Burma is to the west, Laos to the north and east, Cambodia to the southeast, and Malaysia to the south. The south coast of Thailand faces the Gulf of Thailand, while the Isthmus of Kra is bordered on the west by the Andaman Sea (part of the Indian Ocean) and on the east by the Gulf of

Click to Enlarge Image

Thailand. Thailand also has coastal islands in the Andaman Sea and the Gulf of Thailand. The largest, with provincial status, is Phuket, off the west coast; on the gulf side, the largest islands are Samui and Pangan.

Size: Estimates vary. Official Thai sources report 513,115 square kilometers. U.S. government sources state that Thailand has a total of 511,770 square kilometers of land area and 2,230 square kilometers of water area for a total of 514,000 square kilometers.

Land Boundaries: The total land boundary is 4,863 kilometers in length, including borders with Burma (1,800 kilometers), Laos (1,754 kilometers), Cambodia (803 kilometers), and Malaysia (506 kilometers). A dispute between Thailand and Laos over MeKong River islands continues to delay completion of an agreement on the demarcation of their boundary. Thailand has significant differences with Burma over the alignment of their boundary. There are disputed sections of the Thai-Cambodia border where border markers are missing. Land mines, the remnants of former conflicts, are still to be found—sometimes with lethal consequences—along Thailand's borders with Cambodia and Laos. Although Thailand has no actual border dispute with Malaysia, terrorist and insurgent activities in the frontier area lead to frequent border closures and tight security.

Length of Coastline: The coastline is 3,219 kilometers long: 750 kilometers on the Andaman Sea and 2,469 kilometers on the Gulf of Thailand.

Maritime Claims: Thailand claims a 12-nautical-mile territorial sea, a 200-nautical-mile exclusive economic zone, and a continental shelf to a 200-meter depth—or to the depth of exploitation.

Topography: Topography and drainage define four main regions: north, northeast, central, and south. In the north, the chief topographic features are high mountains along the borders with Burma and Laos and extending down the Isthmus of Kra to the southern border with Malaysia. The central plain, which extends to the Gulf of Thailand, is a lowland area drained by the Chao Phraya and its tributary rivers. The upland Khorat Plateau in the northeast drains into the River Mun. The narrow, tropical Isthmus of Kra runs from mainland Thailand to the border with peninsular Malaysia. It has a low-lying range of hills at the narrowest part, about 600 meters in elevation. The highest point is Doi Inthanon, in Chiang Mai Province in northwestern Thailand, at 2,565 meters above sea level. The lowest point is along the Gulf of Thailand at zero meters above sea level.

Principal Rivers: The principal river is the Chao Phraya, which, with its tributaries, drains about 33 percent of the national territory and flows south into a delta at Bangkok. The Mun and many other smaller upland rivers are tributaries of the Mekong, which forms the border between Thailand and Laos before flowing into Cambodia and Vietnam and into the South China Sea. Together, the Chao Phraya and Mekong systems sustain Thailand's agricultural economy and provide waterways for inland navigation.

Climate: A tropical country, Thailand has three distinct seasons. The first is a hot and dry season from February to May, with an average temperature of 34° C and 75 percent relative humidity.

This season is followed by a rainy, cooler season brought by the southwest monsoon from June to September, with an average daily temperature of 29° C and 87 percent relative humidity. A cooler, dry season, caused by the northeast monsoon, lasts from November to January, with temperatures ranging from 32° C to less than 20° C and lower relative humidity. The Isthmus of Kra is always hot and humid and has the heaviest rainfall. The lightest rainfall is in the northeast. Temperatures in Bangkok range between 20° C and 35° C.

Natural Resources: Thailand's major natural resources are fluorite, gypsum, lead, lignite, natural gas, rubber, tantalum, tin, and tungsten. Renewable resources include fish and timber.

Land Use: Roughly 20 percent of Thailand is covered by mountains and hills, the steepness of which generally precludes agriculture. As of 2005, rich arable land accounted for nearly 27.5 percent of the total area. About 6.9 percent was planted to permanent crops. Some 49,860 square kilometers of land were irrigated according to 2003 estimates.

Environmental Factors: The depletion of the water table around Bangkok has led to land subsidence. Despite the annual southwest monsoon, Thailand is subject to drought. Other environmental issues include air pollution from vehicle emissions, water pollution from organic and factory wastes, deforestation, soil erosion, and wildlife population depletion from illegal hunting. Thailand is also vulnerable to devastating tsunamis, such as the one that struck the Andaman Sea coast on December 26, 2004. It killed more than 5,300 people, including foreign visitors, and left another 2,900 missing.

Time Zone: Thailand has one time zone—Bangkok time (Greenwich Mean Time—GMT—plus seven hours).

SOCIETY

Population: Thailand's population was estimated at 64,631,595 in July 2006, making it the nineteenth most populous country in the world. The population growth rate was estimated in 2006 at 0.68 percent. The net migration rate, also based on a 2006 estimate, is 0 percent. In 2005 about 68 percent of the population lived in rural areas and 32 percent in urban areas. The largest population, according to 2000 census data, was in the northeast, with 20.7 million inhabitants and a population density of 122.9 persons per square kilometer. The central region, excluding Bangkok, had the next largest population in 2000, with 14 million inhabitants and a density of 137.8 persons per square kilometer. Bangkok itself had a population of 6.3 million inhabitants and a population density of 4,038 persons per square kilometer. The mountainous north had nearly 11.4 million people, with a density of 67 persons per square kilometer, while the south had 8 million people and a density of 113.9 persons per square kilometer.

Demography: According to estimates of Thailand's age structure for 2006, 22 percent of inhabitants are less than 15 years of age, 70 percent are 15–64 years of age, and 8 percent are 65 and older. Estimates made in 2006 indicate a birthrate of 13.8 births per 1,000 population and a death rate of 7 deaths per 1,000. In 2006 life expectancy was estimated at 74.6 years for women and 69.9 years for men, or nearly 72.2 years total. The infant mortality rate was estimated at nearly 19.4 per 1,000 live births in 2006. The total fertility rate for 2006 has been estimated at nearly 1.6 children per woman.

Ethnic Groups: Official government estimates indicate that people of Thai ethnicity make up 75 percent of the population. Another 14 percent are ethnic Chinese, and 4 percent are Malay, leaving 7 percent as uncategorized. Additionally, as of 2004 Thailand hosted some 188,400 refugees from Burma, many of them ethnic, non-Thai-speaking Karen who fled their country in the face of fighting between Karen rebels and Burmese troops. An estimated 1 million members of hill tribes, collectively called "highlanders," live in the northwest. Remnants of 1940s Chinese Nationalist military forces and their descendants and children of Vietnamese immigrants live in northeastern Thailand.

Languages: Nearly 94 percent of the people speak Tai-Kadai (Daic) languages, with Thai (in various dialects) being predominant and the national and official language. Another 2 percent speak Austro-Asiatic languages, 2 percent speak Austronesian languages, 1 percent speak Tibeto-Burman languages, and 0.2 percent speak Hmong-Mien languages. Standard Thai is based on the dialect spoken in the Chao Phraya Valley. The Thai alphabet, with 44 consonants and 32 vowels, originated during the reign of King Ramkhamhaeng (Rama the Great, r. 1279–98) and is an adaptation of Mon and Khmer scripts derived from Indian Devanagari. Some 74 languages are spoken in Thailand, including numerous Thai dialects plus English, which is the secondary language among the well educated and is widely understood, especially in Bangkok and other large urban areas, where it is a major language of business. Ethnic and regional dialects also are spoken, as are various dialects of Chinese.

Religion: The predominant religion is Theravada Buddhism, representing about 94 percent of the practicing population and about 90 percent of all Thai people. Muslims represent 4.6 percent; Christians, 0.7 percent; Hindus, 0.1 percent; and Sikhs, Baha'i Faith, and others, 0.6 percent. Section 73 of the constitution states that the state shall patronize and protect Buddhism and other religions, promote harmony among the followers of all religions, and encourage the application of religious principles "to create virtue and develop the quality of life." Religious instruction is required in public schools at both the primary and secondary education levels.

Education and Literacy: The Ministry of Education supervises public and private education. Starting in October 2002, the education system offered 12 years of free basic education to students nationwide: six years of primary education beginning at age six or seven, followed by three years of middle school and three years of high school, ending at age 18. Education has been compulsory through the ninth grade (from age seven to 16) since January 2003. With the addition of two years of preprimary schooling, the length of education was extended to 14 years in May 2004. In 2006 an estimated 96 percent of students completed grade six, 80 percent completed grade nine, and 79 percent completed grade 12. In 2004 more than 8.8 million students were enrolled in 32,413 primary, middle, and high schools; 631,000 students were enrolled in 612 vocational education institutions. Thailand also has 20 state universities, 12 of which are in Bangkok, plus 26 private universities and colleges and some 120 other institutions of higher education. Some 1.9 million students were enrolled in postsecondary education in 2003–4. About half of all university graduates were women in 2004. The literacy rate in Thailand is 92.6 percent.

Health: Data on health care are out of date, but in 1995 Thailand had 0.3 physicians and 1.9 hospital beds per 1,000 population. In 2002 annual spending on health care amounted to US$321 per person in purchasing power parity (PPP). Total expenditures represented about 4.4 percent of the gross domestic product (GDP); of this amount, 57.1 percent came from public sources and 42.9 percent from private sources. Some 85 percent of the population had access to potable water in 2002, and 99 percent had access to sanitation. Human immunodeficiency virus/acquired immune deficiency syndrome (HIV/AIDS) is a serious problem in Thailand. The United Nations Programme on HIV/AIDS (UNAIDS) reported in November 2004 that the Thai government had launched a well-funded, politically supported, and pragmatic response to the epidemic. As a result, national adult HIV prevalence has decreased to an estimated 1.5 percent of all persons aged 15 to 49 years (or about 1.8 percent of the total population). It was also reported that 58,000 adults and children had died from AIDS since the first case was reported in 1984. The government has begun to improve its support to persons with HIV/AIDS and has provided funds to HIV/AIDS support groups. Public programs have begun to alter unsafe behavior, but discrimination against those infected continues. The government has funded an antiretroviral drug program and, as of September 2006, more than 80,000 HIV/AIDS patients had received such drugs. Highly pathogenic H5N1 avian influenza (bird flu) has been found among birds in Thailand as well as surrounding areas. The government has pledged financial support for the prevention effort, which mainly focuses on changing poultry farming methods. Major infectious diseases in Thailand also include bacterial diarrhea, hepatitis, dengue fever, malaria, Japanese encephalitis, rabies, and leptospirosis.

Welfare: Thailand has social welfare and social insurance systems. Social welfare involves welfare services aimed at the poor, persons with disabilities, children, the elderly, women, minority hill tribes, and other disadvantaged individuals. The social insurance system provides sickness, maternity, disability, death, dependent child, old age, and unemployment benefits. There also is a social security system for private-sector employees and medical security and pension systems for public-service employees, employees of national enterprises, and military personnel.

ECONOMY

Overview: Thailand's developing, free-enterprise economy has recovered from the Asian financial crisis triggered by speculation against the Thai baht in 1997–98. By 2002 Thailand's standard of living had returned to the level prevailing before the financial crisis. The recovery reflected the benefit of reform measures tied to assistance by the International Monetary Fund, direct investment from Japan, the United States, Singapore, and other nations, and surging exports. During 2001–4 the economy grew at a moderate rate, but the rate of growth was slower than in the booming 1980s and the first half of the 1990s. A long-term shift from agriculture to manufacturing and services continues, but about 39 percent of the workforce is still employed in agriculture, forestry, and fishing, although this sector is responsible for only 10 percent of gross domestic product (GDP). The economy is heavily dependent on exports, such as textiles and computer components, which account for 60 percent of GDP. Between 2002 and 2005, the number of poor declined by around 2 million. In percentage terms, the poverty rate declined from 15.6 percent in 2002 to 12 percent in 2004 and to 9.8 percent in 2005, according to the World Bank.

The military coup that took place on September 19, 2006, has not had a serious impact on the economy. The baht and financial markets experienced brief declines but soon stabilized when investment experts speculated that the coup would help resolve a political standoff that was hurting the economy. Thailand's bond ratings are unchanged; however, credit rating agencies have reported that they may be downgraded depending on future developments. According to investment experts, the economy is strong enough to overcome the temporary disruption caused by the coup.

Gross Domestic Product (GDP): In 2006 Thailand's GDP was US$196.6 billion, reflecting a growth rate of 4.4 percent over 2005. Per capita GDP was US$9,100 using purchasing power parity. In 2006 services constituted 45.2 percent of GDP, followed closely by industry with a 44.9 percent share. Agriculture accounted for the remaining 10 percent.

Government Budget: In 2005 Thailand's central government budget was estimated at US$35.2 billion. The budget was essentially in balance, with a small surplus of around US$467 million.

Inflation: Consumer prices increased by 4.5 percent in 2005, up from 1.8 percent the previous year, partly as a result of global demand for crude oil.

Agriculture, Forestry, and Fishing: In 2006 agriculture, forestry, and fishing contributed less than 10 percent of gross domestic product (GDP) but employed about 39 percent of the workforce. Thailand is the world's leading exporter of rice and a major exporter of shrimp. Other agricultural products include coconuts, corn, rubber, soybeans, sugarcane, and tapioca. In 1985 Thailand officially designated 25 percent of the nation's land area for protected forests and 15 percent for timber production. Protected forests have been set aside for conservation and recreation, while production forests are available for the forestry industry. Between 1992 and 2001, exports of logs and sawn timber increased from 50,000 cubic meters to 2 million cubic meters per year. The regional avian flu outbreak led to a contraction of Thailand's agricultural sector during 2004, and the tsunami disaster of December 26, 2004, devastated the west coast fisheries industry. In 2006 agricultural GDP was estimated to have contracted by 10 percent.

Mining and Minerals: Thailand's major minerals include fluorite, gypsum, lead, lignite, natural gas, rubber, tantalum, tin, and tungsten. The tin mining industry has declined sharply since 1985, and Thailand has gradually become a net importer of tin. As of 2003, the main mineral export was gypsum. Thailand is the world's second largest exporter of gypsum after Canada, even though government policy limits gypsum exports to prevent price cutting. In 2003 Thailand produced more than 40 types of minerals with an annual value of about US$740 million. However, more than 80 percent of these minerals were consumed domestically. In September 2003, in order to encourage foreign investment in the mining industry, the government relaxed severe restrictions on mining by foreign companies and reduced mineral royalties payable to the state.

Industry and Manufacturing: In 2006 industry contributed 44.9 percent of gross domestic product (GDP) but employed only 23 percent of the workforce. This relationship is the opposite of the one applying to agriculture. Industry expanded at an average annual rate of 3.4 percent during the 1995–2004 period. The most important subsector of industry is manufacturing, which accounted for 34.5 percent of GDP in 2004. Thailand is becoming a center of automobile manufacturing for the Association of Southeast Asian Nations (ASEAN) market. By 2004 automobile production had reached 930,000 units, more than twice as much as in 2001. Two automakers active in Thailand are Toyota and Ford. The expansion of the automotive industry has been a boon for domestic steel production. Thailand's electronics industry faces competition from Malaysia and Singapore, while its textile industry faces competition from China and Vietnam.

Energy: In 2004 Thailand's total energy consumption was estimated at 3.4 quadrillion British thermal units, representing about 0.7 percent of total world energy consumption. Thailand is a net importer of oil and natural gas, but the government is promoting the use of ethanol to reduce imports of petroleum and the gasoline additive methyl tertiary butyl ether. In 2005 daily oil consumption of 838,000 barrels per day exceeded domestic production of 306,000 barrels per day. Thailand's four oil refineries have a combined capacity of 703,100 barrels per day. Thailand's government is considering establishing a regional oil processing and transportation hub, serving the needs of south-central China. In 2004 natural gas consumption of 1,055 billion cubic feet exceeded domestic production of 790 billion cubic feet. Also in 2004, estimated coal consumption of 30.4 million short tons exceeded coal production of 22.1 million short tons. As of January 2007, proven oil reserves totaled 290 million barrels, and proven natural gas reserves were 14.8 trillion cubic feet. In 2003 recoverable coal reserves totaled 1,492.5 million short tons.

In 2005 Thailand consumed about 127 billion kilowatt-hours of electricity. Electricity consumption rose by 4.7 percent in 2006 to 133 billion kilowatt-hours. According to the state electricity utility, the Electricity Generating Authority of Thailand, power consumption by residential consumers has been increasing because of more favorable rates given to residential customers over the industry and business sectors. Thailand's state-controlled electric utility and petroleum monopolies are undergoing restructuring.

Services: In 2006 the services sector, which ranges from tourism to banking and finance, contributed 45.2 percent of gross domestic product (GDP) and employed 38 percent of the workforce.

Banking and Finance: Dangerous levels of nonperforming assets at Thai banks helped trigger the attack on the Thai baht by currency speculators that led to the Asian financial crisis in 1997–98. By 2003 nonperforming assets had been cut in half to about 30 percent. Despite a return to profitability, however, Thailand's banks continue to struggle with the legacy of the financial crisis in the form of unrealized losses and inadequate capital. Therefore, the government is considering various reforms, including establishing an integrated financial regulatory agency that would free up the Bank of Thailand to focus on monetary policy. In addition, the Thai government is attempting to strengthen the financial sector through the consolidation of commercial, state-owned, and foreign-owned institutions. Specifically, the government's Financial Sector Reform Master Plan, which was first introduced in early 2004, provides tax breaks to financial institutions that engage in mergers and acquisitions. The reform program has been deemed successful by outside experts. As of 2007, there were three state-owned commercial banks and five state-owned specialized banks, 15 Thai commercial banks, and 17 foreign banks in Thailand.

The Bank of Thailand sought to stem the flow of foreign funds into the country in December 2006. This led within one day to the largest drop in stock prices on the Stock Exchange of Thailand since the 1997 Asian financial crisis. The massive selling by foreign investors amounted more than US$708 million.

Tourism: Tourism makes a larger contribution to Thailand's economy (typically about 6 percent of gross domestic product) than that of any other Asian nation. In 2004 some 11 million tourists visited Thailand. However, terrorism in southern Thailand and in Indonesia and natural disasters, most notably the December 2004 tsunami, have taken their toll on tourism. One of the negative side effects of Thailand's tourism industry is a burgeoning sex tourism industry and a related threat from human immunodeficiency virus/acquired immune deficiency syndrome (HIV/AIDS).

Labor: Thailand's labor force was estimated at 35.5 million in 2006. About 39 percent were employed in agriculture, 38 percent in services, and 23 percent in industry. In 2005 women constituted 48 percent of the labor force and held an increasing share of professional jobs. Less than 4 percent of the workforce is unionized, but 11 percent of industrial workers and 50 percent of state enterprise employees are unionized. Although laws applying to private-sector workers' rights to form and join trade unions were unaffected by the September 19, 2006, military coup and its aftermath, workers who participate in union activities continue to have inadequate legal protection. According to the U.S. Department of State, union workers are inadequately protected. In 2006 Thailand's unemployment rate was 2.1 percent of the labor force.

Foreign Economic Relations: Thailand seeks expanded trade through free-trade agreements and multilateral cooperation within such organizations as the Asian Development Bank, Asia-Pacific Economic Cooperation, Association of Southeast Asian Nations, and World Trade Organization. Under the auspices of the Asian Development Bank, Thailand joined the Greater Mekong Subregion's development program in 1992. Japan and the United States are Thailand's top two trading partners and sources of direct investment. Thailand grants the United States preferential treatment for investment under the Thai-U.S. Treaty of Amity and Economic Relations of 1966. Despite close economic ties between Thailand and the United States, the relationship suffers from disputes over agricultural trade, intellectual property rights, and customs procedures. In July 2005, Thailand reached bilateral free-trade agreements with key trading partners, such as Australia, New Zealand, China, India, and Bahrain. However, the trade deals were unpopular with domestic political opponents of the Thaksin Chinnawat government (2001–6) who claimed that the agreements failed to sufficiently protect Thai interests. China is gaining importance as a trading partner and competitor for foreign direct investment and export markets, particularly in the areas of agriculture, computer hardware, and textiles.

Imports: In 2006 Thailand imported US$125.9 billion of goods, including raw materials and intermediates (US$51.9 billion), capital goods (US$33.1 billion), fuel and lubricants (US$25.4 billion), consumer goods (US$9.5 billion), and consumer durables, such as electrical appliances

(US$6 billion). Thailand's principal import partners in 2006 were Japan (20.4 percent), China (10.6 percent), the United States (6.7 percent), Malaysia (6.6 percent), and the United Arab Emirates (4.8 percent).

Exports: In 2005 Thailand exported US$109.2 billion of goods. Most exports related to manufacturing, including machinery and mechanical appliances (US$16.1 billion), electrical apparatus for circuits (US$8.9 billion), integrated circuits and parts (US$5.5 billion), and textiles (US$5.5 billion). Thailand's principal export partners in 2005 were the United States (15.4 percent), Japan (13.7 percent), China (8.3 percent), Singapore (6.8 percent), and Hong Kong (5.6 percent).

Trade Balance: In 2006 Thailand posted a merchandise trade surplus of US$2.3 billion.

Balance of Payments: In 2005 Thailand had a negative current account balance of US$3.7 billion. This deficit reflected the deterioration in the merchandise trade account, mainly because of a sharp rise in the import bill. According to an International Monetary Fund report, the current account deficit stood at US$3.7 billion in 2005.

External Debt: As of June 2006, total external debt was US$57.83 billion, or about 34 percent of gross domestic product (GDP). Foreign exchange reserves, once depleted during the financial crisis of 1997–98, increased steadily to US$41 billion in 2003, US$51 billion in 2004, US$52 billion in 2005, and US$59 billion in 2006.

Foreign Investment: In 2005 foreign direct investment was inbound US$3.3 billion. The largest foreign investors were the United States, Japan, Singapore, and the European Union.

Foreign Aid: On July 31, 2003, Thailand repaid its outstanding obligations under a standby arrangement from the International Monetary Fund designed to help it recover from the 1997–98 Asian financial crisis. Payment was made one year ahead of schedule, reflecting the achievement of macroeconomic and balance-of-payments stability. In 2005 the World Bank was funding eight development projects in Thailand. These projects encompassed the areas of social investment (US$300 million), education (US$225 million), land titling (US$118 million), technical assistance (US$30 million), and energy (US$245 million). Despite the devastating tsunami of December 26, 2004, the Thai government announced it did not need any international financial assistance in response.

Currency and Exchange Rate: Thailand's currency is the baht. On July 11, 2007, one U.S. dollar was equivalent to 31.74 Thai baht. Currency is issued in 10, 20, 50, 100, 500, and 1,000 baht notes. Coins are minted in 25 and 50 satang and 1, 5, and 10 baht denominations.

Fiscal Year: October 1 to September 30.

TRANSPORTATION AND TELECOMMUNICATIONS

Overview: Where topography allows it, Thailand has an extensive network of roads and railroads. Rapid transit is burgeoning in an otherwise gridlocked Bangkok. Tourism and improved economic development led Bangkok to become a major regional air hub. New technology development has brought some improvements to the nation's telecommunications network.

Roads: Estimates vary on the length of roads in Thailand. According to a U.S. government estimate in 2000, Thailand had 57,403 kilometers of roads, 56,542 kilometers of which were paved and 861 kilometers, unpaved. Other sources indicate a lower total of fewer than 45,000 kilometers. Streets in Bangkok are frequently gridlocked, with an overabundance of motor vehicles flowing into the central city via expressways.

Railroads: Railroads are operated under the auspices of the State Railway of Thailand. In 2005 the system totaled an estimated 4,071 kilometers of narrow-gauge (1.000-meter gauge) track. The system currently has some 270 diesel locomotives and nearly 250 diesel railcars or multiple-unit cars. According to figures provided for 2002, 55.7 million passenger journeys occurred, and the rail system hauled 9.9 million tons of freight. Freight traffic is considered an important part of Thailand's domestic container transport to and from seaport and inland terminals.

Rapid Transit: The Mass Rapid Transit Authority of Thailand operates a full metro service on a 21-kilometer-long, 18-station line that opened in Bangkok in 2004. The inaugural line will be extended in phases totaling 27 kilometers, and two future lines, totaling 67 kilometers, are planned.

Ports: Thailand's ports in order of size are Bangkok, Laem Chabang, Pattani, Phuket, Sattahip, Si Racha, and Songkhla. The Thai merchant fleet comprises 400 ships of 1,000 gross registered tons or more, including 145 cargo carriers, 91 petroleum tankers, 60 bulk carriers, 32 refrigerated cargo ships, 29 liquefied gas ships, 21 container ships, 14 chemical tankers, 6 passenger/cargo ships, 1 passenger ship, and 1 specialized tanker.

Inland and Coastal Waterways: Thailand has some 4,000 kilometers of navigable inland waterways, 92 percent of which, or 3,701 kilometers, are navigable by boats with drafts up to 0.9 meters. Thailand's long coastlines lend themselves to intercoastal trade.

Civil Aviation and Airports: In 2006 Thailand had an estimated 108 airports and three heliports. Sixty-six of the airports had paved runways, including eight of more than 3,047 meters in length. Bangkok International Airport at Don Muang, 24 kilometers north of the capital, is an important regional hub for pass-through flights and as a destination. About 80 airlines provide service to the Bangkok International Airport and carry a reported 25 million passengers and 700,000 tons of cargo a year. Ground was broken for a new Bangkok international airport at Suwannabhumi, 30 kilometers east of Bangkok, in January 2002, with a new projected opening in 2006. When Suwannabhumi opens, Don Muang will be used for domestic flights only. Other major airports are at Chiangmai, Hat Yai, and Pattani. There are two Thai flag carriers. Thai Airways International, founded in 1960, offers domestic and worldwide coverage with a fleet of

81 passenger and cargo aircraft. Since 1977, Thai Airways has been fully owned by the Thai government. Bangkok Airways is a privately owned company founded in 1968 as an air taxi company; since 1986, it has served primarily as a domestic carrier. It also flies to Phnom Penh, Cambodia, and offers charter flights to Burma; it has a fleet of 11 aircraft.

Pipelines: In 2006 Thailand had 3,760 kilometers of gas pipelines and 379 kilometers of refined products pipelines.

Telecommunications: In 2002 the Thai government formed a new Ministry of Information and Communications to oversee all aspects of telecommunications. By 2006 the ministry was to have liberalized the provision of telecommunications services under World Trade Organization guidelines. However, the proposed privatization of the state-owned Telephone Organization of Thailand and Communications Authority of Thailand remains controversial. The ministry also is responsible for implementing the country's information technology policy, called IT 2010, which is designed to strengthen Thailand's telecommunications infrastructure as a means of promoting overall economic development.

Thailand's telecommunications network suffers from delays and other shortfalls in the provision of telephone services as a result of inadequate investment. The quality and availability of telephone service are much better in Bangkok and other cities than in rural areas. Mobile telephones (27.3 million in 2005) are much more prevalent than landline phones (6.7 million in 2004). In 2005 Thailand had 8.4 million Internet users, representing less than 11 percent of the population.

State entities, including the police and military, and government allies own almost all television and radio stations and play an important role in determining programming content. The government's Public Relations Department requires that all Thai radio stations carry 30 minutes of official news prepared by Radio Thailand, the government's national radio network, twice daily. Radio Thailand has seven networks that specialize in such areas as news and information, public affairs, social issues, education, and foreign-language broadcasts. Thailand has five television channels, two of which are run by the central government, two by the army, and one by a private enterprise. Altogether, Thailand has 204 AM radio stations, 334 FM radio stations, 6 shortwave stations, and 111 television broadcast stations. Additionally, there are between 2,000 and 3,000 community radio stations, many of which operate outside the law by using frequencies restricted to government entities. Those that register are allowed to continue broadcasting but others, including those critical of the government, have been shut down. Thailand has about 14 million radios and 15 million television sets.

GOVERNMENT AND POLITICS

Government Overview: Thailand is a constitutional monarchy with, until September 19, 2006, a democratically elected bicameral legislature. On September 19, a military junta led by the commander in chief of the Thai army, Lieutenant General Sonthi Bunyaratklin, ousted the elected government of Prime Minister Thaksin Shinawatra. When the coup was staged in Bangkok, Thaksin himself was in New York City to address the opening session of the United

Nations General Assembly. He attempted to issue a martial law decree and demanded Sonthi's arrest. The response was the establishment of the Council for Democratic Reform under Sonthi's chairmanship, suspension of the 1997 constitution, a crackdown on the open media, and detention of cabinet members and political opponents of the military regime. On the day of the coup, King Bhumibol Adulyadej and Queen Sirikit met with coup leaders, and on September 21 the king officially appointed Sonthi as chairman of the military authorities, known as the Council for National Security (CNS).

An interim 39-article constitution drafted by the council was endorsed by King Bhumibol and promulgated on October 1, 2006. It is to remain in place until a permanent constitution is proclaimed, prior to legislative elections scheduled for October 2007. The interim constitution gives overwhelming power to the executive branch and the CNS, with the CNS chairman having the power to appoint and remove the prime minister. Although the details of the permanent constitution are not yet known, internal observers predicted that it will restrict the economic and political authority of the prime minister and more closely delineate the powers of the monarchy, military, and parliament.

Whereas previous governments had relied on fragile coalitions, since becoming prime minister in 2001, Thaksin Shinawatra had steadily increased his parliamentary power by forging alliances with other parties and attracting members of other parties to his Thai Rak Thai Party (Thai Loves Thai Party). The Thai Rak Thai's continuous success in national elections allowed it to assume a more dominant position in government and to dictate policy much more easily. Opposition parties, such as the Phak Prachathipat Party (Democratic Party), were greatly weakened, while coalition parties, such as the Phak Chat Thai Party (Thai Nation Party) and Pak Khwam Wang Mei (New Aspiration Party), were merged with the Thai Rak Thai. In the elections of February 2005, the Thai Rak Thai won 377 out of 500 seats, and for the first time in its history Thailand formed a democratically elected one-party government. The Thai Rak Thai's growing domination engendered deep concerns over Thaksin's overwhelming power and influence. In particular, objections frequently were raised about his tendency to reorganize the government and to reshuffle the cabinet with his personal friends and family members. After coming to power, Thaksin instituted 12 cabinet shuffles, the most recent in August 2005. Public and parliamentary criticism of Thaksin's regime eventually led to mass demonstrations in the latter months of 2005 and early 2006 and dissolution of parliament by Thaksin on February 24, 2006. Consequently, new elections were held on April 2, 2006. However, Thailand's Constitutional Court invalidated the results after the opposition parties refused to compete against Thaksin's Thai Rak Thai.

On August 24, 2006, police intercepted an explosives-laden automobile, operated by a former driver in the Internal Security Operations Command, near Thaksin's residence in Thonburi. Although critics accused Thaksin of fabricating the plot to boost his popularity in the upcoming October general elections, five army officers were arrested for their role in the plot. Three of them were released after the military overthrew the Thaksin government in September. According to a white paper issued by the CNS in November 2006, causes of the coup were corruption, abuse of power, lack of integrity, interference in the checks and balances system, human rights violations, and destroying the unity of the people during the leadership of the Thaksin government.

Political opposition leaders and pro-democracy advocates initially embraced the September 19 coup. However, the CNS's popularity declined following an escalation of violence with Islamic separatists in the south, a series of bombings in Bangkok, slow progress on a new constitution, and the adoption of populist economic measures and capital controls that have alarmed foreign investors. On January 31, 2007, General Sonthi made a public announcement that he would hold democratic elections before the end of the year. He also promised that the army would immediately hand over control to a civilian government following the inauguration of a new prime minister.

Executive Branch: The constitutional monarch and head of state, since June 9, 1946, is King Bhumibol Adulyadej (Rama IX of the Chakri Dynasty). The Privy Council, which is still provided for in the interim constitution, is an 18-member constitutional body that advises the king on matters of legislation, government affairs, clemency, awards, and other matters requiring the king's signature. The Privy Council, whose members are appointed by and serve at the pleasure of the king, also recommends the name of a suitable person to hold the position of regent when the king is absent from Thailand or unable to perform his duties. Under the interim constitution, executive governmental power is exercised through a cabinet headed by a prime minister appointed by the king (with the concurrence of the Council for National Security (CNS) chairman) and the 19 members of the Council of Ministers who head major ministries. However, the military coup in September 2006 abolished the cabinet and installed the Council for Democratic Reform. The first appointments to the council were the supreme commander of the armed forces, Boonsrang Naimpradit, the three military service chiefs of staff, the police commissioner, and the secretary general of the CNS. The interim prime minister (since October 1, 2006) is Surayut Chulanon, a retired general and privy councilor to King Bhumibol.

Legislative Branch: Prior to the September 2006 military coup, legislative power was exercised through a bicameral National Assembly composed of the House of Representatives (Saphaputhan Ratsadon) and Senate (Wuthisapha). All legislative matters of national policy received the approval of the National Assembly and the signature of the king before becoming law. Members of both houses served four-year terms. The number of representatives was determined by the size of the population. At the time of the coup, House membership stood at 500; 100 members were elected from a party list and 400 on a constituency basis. According to the 1997 constitution, the Senate was an appointed body until members were elected in single-seat constituencies for the first time in March 2000. The 200 members of the Senate had to have attained the minimum age of 40 and not belong to any political party in any capacity. The constitution also stated that the number of senators should not exceed 75 percent of the total number of representatives. Upon assuming control in September 2006, the Council for National Security (CNS) dissolved both chambers of the National Assembly and subsequently arranged for the king to appoint a new 242-member (250 are authorized by the interim constitution) legislature, a significant proportion of which was composed of retired government officials and members of the military. In accordance with Article 7 of the interim constitution, the CNS chairman countersigns the king's appointments to the National Assembly. The new National Assembly, which serves as both the House of Representatives and the Senate, was charged with governing the country in the period leading up to the general elections scheduled for October 2007.

Judicial Branch: Following the September 19, 2006, military coup and the repeal of the 1997 constitution, the Council for National Security issued a decree announcing that all courts with the exception of the Constitutional Court (which was dissolved) would continue to operate as before. The interim constitution, promulgated on October 1, 2006, guarantees the independence of the judiciary. Thailand has a three-level court system collectively known as the Courts of Justice. At the top is the Supreme Court of Justice. Below it are the Court of Appeal and, at the third level, the Courts of First Instance, over which the Supreme Administrative Court, which was established in 1999, presides. The Courts of First Instance include the Central Administrative Court and 16 regional administrative courts. A new Constitutional Tribunal, composed of justices from the Supreme Court of Justice and the Supreme Administrative Court, was established on October 1, 2006, to replace the functions of the Constitutional Court. Judges of the Supreme Court of Justice and the Supreme Administrative Court are subject to Senate approval. Other judges are members of the career civil service and are not subject to parliamentary review. Separate administrative courts adjudicate disputes involving state agencies, state enterprises, and local government organizations or between state officials and private individuals. Administrative appellate and supreme administrative courts operate at higher levels. A separate Military Court deals with military personnel and persons arrested during periods of martial law. Islamic sharia courts hear civil cases involving members of the Muslim minority.

Administrative Divisions: Thailand has 76 provinces (*changwat*), including Bangkok Municipality. The provinces are divided into 795 districts (*amphoe*), 81 subdistricts (*king amphoe*), 7,255 rural administrative subdistricts (*tambon*), and 69,866 villages (*muban*).

Provincial and Local Government: Local government is based on the principles of decentralization and self-government when certain legal conditions are met. Under the 1997 constitution, elected local assemblies and elected or appointed local administrative committees were allowed four-year terms. Central government officials could not serve as local officials. Bangkok is a provincial-level entity with an elected governor and the legislative Metropolitan Administration Council. Supervision of provincial and local government takes place through the Department of Local Administration of the Ministry of Interior. However, as a result of the September 2006 military coup, Bangkok and the provinces came under the direct control of the supreme commander of the armed forces and the national police.

Judicial and Legal System: The interim constitution of October 1, 2006, had been criticized by many internal observers for granting legal authority to the junta's postcoup announcements and orders, including bans against demonstrations and political activities. Until the coup, the Thai legal system had been based on an amalgam of traditional and modern laws and customs, including Islamic law, where applicable. Most of the modern legal system is based on criminal, civil, and commercial codes adopted from the British and other European legal systems, along with borrowings from India, China, Japan, and the United States. Traditional civil rights were protected under the old constitution, but even under the old constitution there was no trial by jury. A single judge decided trials for misdemeanors; two or more judges were required for more serious cases. The 1997 constitution also provided for the presumption of innocence, and criminal detainees were guaranteed access to legal counsel; however, local police have been accused of ignoring this procedure and conducting interrogations of suspects without providing access to an attorney. Regulations outlined in the Criminal Code require public prosecutors to rely exclusively on the recommendations of the police when determining whether to bring a case forward for criminal prosecution. Police are required to bring criminal cases to prosecutors for the filing of court charges within 48 hours of arrest. Extensions of up to three days are permitted, and police, with court permission, may hold suspects for up to 82 days for serious offenses while investigations are being conducted.

Electoral System: There are no elections for the heads of state and government. The monarchy is hereditary and based on the Palace Law of Succession enacted in 1924, which allows the king to appoint his heir. If he has failed to do so, the Privy Council nominates an heir for National Assembly consideration. The heir suggested by the Privy Council may be a prince or princess. Under the 1997 constitution, the prime minister was selected from among the members of the House of Representatives following elections. Officially, the king appoints the prime minister, who, before the September 2006 coup, was normally the leader of the party that had an outright majority or organized a majority coalition in the House of Representatives. The Senate also was elected by popular vote for nonparty candidates.

Politics and Political Parties: Active political parties include the Phak Prachathipat Party (Democratic Party); Phak Mahachon Party (Great People's Party); Phak Chat Thai Party (Thai Nation Party); and Thai Rak Thai Party (Thai Loves Thai Party). After the September 2006 military coup, new elections were scheduled for October 2007.

Mass Media: The Thai media are generally free but even before the September 19, 2006, military coup had acted with restraint because of fear of lawsuits and, from time to time, government censorship. In the aftermath of the September coup, the military quickly clamped down on the media and banned political gatherings of more than five people, but it subsequently lifted its restrictions. Since then the Thai press has routinely published critical commentary on the military and covered Thaksin Chinnawat's travel movements in exile. However, the government ordered the Thai broadcast media to cease reporting statements by Thaksin and to stop airing views defending the former prime minister. There are 18 major Thai-language daily newspapers, 3 major English-language dailies, and 4 major Chinese-language dailies. Thailand also has 204 AM radio stations, 334 FM radio stations, 6 shortwave stations, and 111 television broadcast stations.

Foreign Relations: According to the foreign policy statement issued by the interim government in November 2006, Thailand's foreign policy includes support for the Association of Southeast Asian Nations (ASEAN) in the interest of regional stability and emphasis on a close and long-standing security relationship with the United States. Since the 1990s, Thailand has taken an increasingly active role on the international stage. When East Timor gained independence from Indonesia, Thailand, for the first time in its history, contributed troops to the international peacekeeping effort. As part of its effort to improve international ties, Thailand has sought observer status in such regional organizations as the Organization of American States (OAS) and the Organization for Security and Co-operation in Europe (OSCE).

Despite the widespread international condemnation of the September 19, 2006, military-led coup, Thailand's relations with its allies have not been seriously affected. The U.S. ambassador to Thailand met with coup leader General Surayud Chulanont on October 2, 2006, and reported that he had been assured that the military-installed civilian government would protect civil liberties and move toward a quick return to a democratically elected administration. However, foreign observers also predicted that if there are delays in the restoration of civilian government, relations between the United States and Thailand could take a turn for the worse. This would also likely be the case with the European Union and Australia, which expressed concerns about the coup and called for a speedy return to democratic rule.

Membership in International Organizations: Thailand belongs to the following international organizations: Asia-Pacific Economic Cooperation, Asia-Pacific Telecommunity, Asian Development Bank, Asian Institute of Technology, Asian-Pacific Postal Training Centre, Asian Reinsurance Corporation, Association of Southeast Asian Nations (ASEAN) and the ASEAN Regional Forum, Bank for International Settlements, Colombo Plan, Committee for Coordination of Joint Prospecting for Mineral Resources in Asian Offshore Areas, Group of 77, International Atomic Energy Agency, International Chamber of Commerce, International Committee of the Red Cross, International Confederation of Free Trade Unions, International Criminal Court, International Criminal Police Organization, International Federation of Red Cross and Red Crescent Societies, International Hydrographic Organization, International Olympic Committee, International Organization for Migration, International Organization for Standardization, International Red Cross and Red Crescent Movement, Mekong River Commission, Network of Aquaculture Centres in Asia-Pacific, Nonaligned Movement, Organisation for the Prohibition of Chemical Weapons, Organization for Security and Co-operation in Europe (partner), Organization of American States (observer), Organization of the Islamic Conference (observer), Permanent Court of Arbitration, Southeast Asian Fisheries Development Center, Southeast Asian Ministers of Education Secretariat, World Confederation of Labor, World Customs Organization, World Federation of Trade Unions, World Tourism Organization, and World Trade Organization. Within the United Nations (UN) system, Thailand is a member of the Economic and Social Commission for Asia and the Pacific (ESCAP); Food and Agriculture Organization (FAO); International Bank for Reconstruction and Development (IBRD); International Civil Aviation Organization (ICAO); International Development Association (IDA); International Finance Corporation (IFC); International Fund for Agricultural Development (IFAD); International Labour Organization (ILO); International Maritime Organization (IMO); International Monetary Fund (IMF); International Telecommunication Union (ITU); Multilateral Investment Guarantee Agency (MIGA); UN Children's Fund (UNICEF); UN Conference on Trade and Development (UNCTAD); UN Development Fund for Women (UNIFEM); UN Development Programme (UNDP); UN Educational, Scientific, and Cultural Organization (UNESCO); UN Environment Programme (UNEP); UN Industrial Development Organization (UNIDO); UN Office for Asia of the United Nations Office for Project Services; UN Office of the High Commissioner for Refugees (UNHCR); UN Office on Drugs and Crime; UN Population Fund (UNFPA); UN Regional Center for East Asia and the Pacific; Universal Postal Union (UPU); World Health Organization (WHO); World Intellectual Property Organization (WIPO); and World Meteorological Organization (WMO).

Major International Treaties: Thailand is a signatory to the Biological Weapons Convention; Chemical Weapons Convention; Geneva Protocol for the Prohibition of the Use in War of Asphyxiating, Poisonous, or Other Gases, and of Bacteriological Methods of Warfare; Treaty

Banning Nuclear Weapon Tests in the Atmosphere, in Outer Space, and Under Water; Treaty on the Nonproliferation of Nuclear Weapons; and Treaty on Principles Governing the Activities of States in the Exploration and Use of Outer Space, Including the Moon and Other Celestial Bodies. Thailand also is a party to the Biodiversity, Climate Change, Climate Change–Kyoto Protocol, Desertification, Endangered Species, Hazardous Waste, Marine Life Conservation, Ozone Layer Protection, Tropical Timber 83, Tropical Timber 94, and Wetlands environmental agreements. It has signed but not ratified the United Nations Law of the Sea Treaty.

NATIONAL SECURITY

Armed Forces Overview: The military includes three branches: the Royal Thai Army (123,000), the Royal Thai Navy (77,000, including 2,000 naval aviation personnel and 27,000 members of the Royal Thai Marine Corps), and the Royal Thai Air Force (estimated at 47,500). Reserve forces total 200,000 personnel. Under normal operating circumstances, the minister of defense and the supreme commander of the armed forces are at the top of the chain of command and maintain control; however, real power is held by the three service chiefs. Since the September 19, 2006, coup, the army commander in chief has been dominant, and it is unclear what the chain of command is and how it might change in the future.

Foreign Military Relations: A long-standing ally of the United States, Thailand signed numerous bilateral defense and mutual security agreements between 1950 and 2003. In 2002 Thailand received Foreign Military Assistance from the United States in the amount of US$3 million; in 2003 it received US$3.7 million; in 2004, US$3.4 million; and in 2005, US$1.4 million. Most Thai military equipment is from the United States, the United Kingdom, and China.

External Threat: Thailand faces a number of external threats from cross-border activities. Those on the border with Burma involve the handling of ethnic rebels, refugees, and illegal crossings, often related to drugs and arms trafficking. There have been periodic armed border clashes between Thai and Burmese border guards. Some 98,000 Karen refugees live in camps on the Thai side of the Burma–Thailand border, and rebel members of this group have skirmished with Thai troops. In 2001 and 2002, Thai and pro-Rangoon forces clashed in Thai territory, leading to strained relations between the two nations. Similarly, separatist insurgents in predominantly Muslim southern Thailand allegedly have operated from neighboring Malaysia, leading to cooperation between the two governments and Malaysian arrests of separatist ringleaders. Thailand has periodically closed border areas where communist Cambodian insurgents at odds with the Phnom Penh government control neighboring territory. The Cambodian government has accused Thailand of complicity with the insurgents.

Defense Budget: Defense expenditures in fiscal year (FY) 2006 were estimated at US$2 billion, representing 1.09 percent of the gross domestic product (GDP). The military-backed administration that came to power following the September 2006 coup endorsed an almost 35 percent increase in the defense budget for FY 2007. A Ministry of Defense spokesperson said additional funding was needed to make up for shortfalls accumulated during Thaksin Shinawatra's five-year rule, expand the counterinsurgency campaign in the southern provinces, replace or refurbish equipment, and replenish ammunition, stores, and fuel stocks. The projected defense budget for FY 2007 was US$3.2 billion.

Major Military Units: The army has four regional armies, two corps, three armored infantry divisions, two cavalry divisions, two mechanized infantry divisions, two special forces divisions, one artillery division, one air defense artillery division, one engineer division, one economic development division, one independent cavalry regiment, eight independent infantry battalions, four reconnaissance companies, and one armored air cavalry regiment. Four rapid-reaction force battalions are being formed, and there are four reserve infantry divisions. The navy has three fleets (North Gulf, South Gulf, and Andaman Sea), one naval air division, and five naval bases (including one supporting its Mekong River Operating Unit). The marines are organized into one division with two infantry regiments, one artillery regiment, one amphibious assault battalion, and one reconnaissance battalion. The air force is organized into four air divisions.

Major Military Equipment: The army has between 330 and 380 main battle tanks of various types, between 210 and 460 light tanks (some in storage), 32 reconnaissance vehicles, about 950 armored personnel carriers, 550 pieces of towed artillery, 20 pieces of self-propelled artillery, 1,900 mortars, more than 320 air defense guns, and an arsenal of antitank guided weapons, rocket launchers, recoilless launchers, and surface-to-air missiles. The army also has an unmanned autonomous search vehicle, a variety of fixed-wing aircraft, 3 attack helicopters, 158 transport helicopters, and 40 training helicopters. The navy has 1 aircraft carrier, 12 frigates, 5 corvettes, 6 fast attack craft armed with missiles, 15 patrol craft, 7 mine warfare ships, 7 amphibious forces ships, and 15 support and miscellaneous ships. Naval aviation has 27 combat aircraft, 1 antisubmarine warfare aircraft, 24 maritime air patrol planes, 2 transports, 2 search-and-rescue planes, 14 antisubmarine warfare helicopters, 5 search-and-rescue helicopters, and 6 transport helicopters. The marine corps has 33 assault amphibian vehicles, 24 armored personnel carriers, 48 pieces of towed artillery, 14 air defense guns, and 24 or more antitank guided weapons. The air force has 194 combat aircraft, 1 electronic intelligence aircraft, 3 reconnaissance aircraft, 2 survey planes, 38 transport aircraft, and a small fleet of aircraft used by the king and other VIPs as well as aircraft used for liaison purposes. Although the air force has no armed helicopters, it does have 34 unarmed helicopters. On the ground, the air force has one antiaircraft artillery battalion and surface-to-air missile forces.

Military Service: Men reaching 21 years of age are subject to two years of compulsory military service. Volunteers may join at the minimum age of 18. Women may also join the military, but they are not accepted in the police or military academies. They do serve, however, as military academy instructors.

Paramilitary Forces: Thailand has about 113,700 active-duty paramilitary personnel. These forces include about 20,000 members of a light infantry force called the Thahan Phran (Hunter Soldiers or Royal Thai Rangers), which was organized in 1978 to fight communist guerrillas and is now deployed in active troublespots along the border. The 45,000-strong Volunteer Defense Corps provides the border patrol police with law and order support during military emergencies and natural disasters.

Foreign Military Forces: The United States has 30 air force, 10 navy, and 29 marine corps personnel station in Thailand.

Military Forces Abroad: Thailand had about 500 troops in Iraq from October 2003 to September 2004 and also sent a small contingent to Afghanistan. Since 2000, Thailand has sent observers, police, and troops to the following United Nations (UN) multinational peacekeeping operations: UN Iraq–Kuwait Observer Mission (UNIKOM), UN Mission in Bosnia Herzegovina (UNMIBH), and UN Transitional Administration in East Timor (UNTAET). As of January 31, 2007, Thailand had 12 military observers with the United Nations Mission in Sudan (UNMIS) and 31 police officers with the United Nations Mission in East Timor (UNMIT).

Police and Internal Security: The Royal Thai Police have approximately 213,000 officers organized in 10 geographic regions. These forces include provincial police, marine police, police aviation, and border patrol police. The national police are under the command of the police commissioner general, who reports directly to the prime minister—a member of the military junta—and the 20-member Police Commission. The police commissioner general is appointed by the prime minister, subject to cabinet and royal approval. The Border Patrol Police have special authority and responsibility in border areas to combat insurgent and separatist movements. Thailand also has a Central Police Academy and provincial police training schools.

Terrorism: Since the September 11, 2001, terrorist attacks on the United States, Thailand has pledged itself as a strong ally in the United States–led war on terrorism. Thailand itself has been confronted with terrorist violence, primarily in the predominantly Muslim southern provinces of Narathiwat, Pattani, and Yala, which border Malaysia. In 2002 Thai police officers were killed and bombs were detonated when the minister of interior toured the violence-prone area; five schools suffered damage from arsonists. The Thai military attributed these actions to Guragan Mujahideen Islam Pattani (Pattani Islamic Mujahideen Movement), thought to be an al Qaeda affiliate, which was established in 1995 as a constituent group of Bersatu (United Front for the Independence of Pattani). Bersatu was established in 1989, and both organizations have the goal of establishing a Muslim state in southern Thailand.

In 2003 suspected members of Jemaah Islamiah (Community of Islam, a regional group affiliated with al Qaeda, established in 1993 or 1994), who were arrested in June 2003, confessed to plotting attacks on embassies in Bangkok and tourist sites. Further arsons and bombings and attacks on police and army bases in 2004 heightened the terrorist threat. When seven Muslim protesters were shot and 78 others died in police custody in October 2004, 30 Buddhists were killed in November in retaliation. In 2004 alone, more than 500 people died as a result of insurgent and terrorist violence in the south. This separatist violence has led to border closures and security tightening with neighboring Malaysia to inhibit terrorist activities. During 2006 violence in the southern provinces, and particularly violence aimed at public school teachers, sporadically forced the temporary closure of public schools and disrupted the educational process in those areas. Fears of terrorism against Thailand's own tourist resorts emanated from the terrorist bombings in Bali, Indonesia, in October 2002. There were allegations that the Bali bombers, members of Jemaah Islamiah, may have planned their attack while living in southern Thailand.

On December 31, 2006, and January 1, 2007, four bombs exploded in Bangkok, followed by several more explosions in various parts of the city, killing at least three people and injuring more than 38. Prime Minister Surayut Chulanon said that the bombs were designed to resemble those used by the southern insurgents. However, it was announced later that closer inspection confirmed that there was no link. On January 20, 2007, police announced that 15 military officers and civilians had been arrested related to the bombing incident. General Sonthi, head of the junta, strongly criticized the chief of police for seeking scapegoats within the military, claiming that the 15 suspects had no connection to the incident.

Human Rights: Following the September 19, 2006, military coup, the Council for National Security—the junta's ruling body—imposed some limits on freedom of speech, freedom of the press, and freedom of assembly. Prior to the coup, the government under the now-abrogated 1997 constitution, generally respected the human rights of its citizens. Some significant problems, however, continued under the interim government. During 2006, according to the U.S. Department of State's *Country Reports on Human Rights Practices*, "security forces continued to use excessive force against criminal suspects and committed or were connected to dozens of extrajudicial, arbitrary, and unlawful killings." There also were reports that disappearances continued in the southern provinces, particularly after the missing allegedly had been questioned by security officials. There also were reports that police tortured, beat, and otherwise abused detainees and prisoners, generally with impunity. Authorities used defamation suits and, in some cases, charges of sedition against critics, which led to self-censorship by the media and nongovernmental organizations. Human rights workers, particularly those focusing on disappearances and the violence in the south, experienced government harassment. Thailand continued to be a source, transit point, and destination for trafficking in women and children for a variety of purposes, including indentured servitude, forced labor, and prostitution. Members of hill tribes without proper documentation continued to face restrictions on their movement, could not own land, and were not protected by labor laws.

Trafficking in women and children and forced prostitution and labor are serious problems in Thailand. It is conservatively estimated that between 200,000 and 300,000 men, women, and children—but particularly women and young girls—are engaged in prostitution as part of Thailand's illegal sex tourism industry. Of these, between 30,000 and 40,000 prostitutes are under the age of 18 years; this figure does not include foreign migrants, many of whom come from Burma, Cambodia, China, and Laos. Thai and migrant women also are trafficked to Japan, Malaysia, Singapore, Bahrain, Australia, South Africa, Europe, and the United States for prostitution and sweatshop labor. Men, women, and children from China and Southeast Asian neighbors also are trafficked for sweatshop, fishery, construction, farm, and industrial labor.